EVERYDAY HICCUPS & CHALLENGES

I hope you enjoy this lovely book & being a part of this adventure.
Lots of Love,

Amanda

Amanda Spiteri
Everyday Hiccups & Challenges

Published by BooxAi
ISBN: 978-965-578-662-0

BooX AI

.

EVERYDAY HICCUPS & CHALLENGES

GUIDING YOU THROUGH REAL-LIFE ADVENTURES

AMANDA SPITERI

INDEX

INTRODUCTION

Hey, kids! Before we dive into our fun book and activities, let's talk about something really cool – our feelings and how our brains are like superheroes that help us handle them!

1. The Brain as a Control Centre:

Think of your brain as a control centre. It's like the boss of your body and your feelings. Your brain helps you see, hear, taste, and feel things. But it's also in charge of your emotions – like when you're happy, sad, or excited!

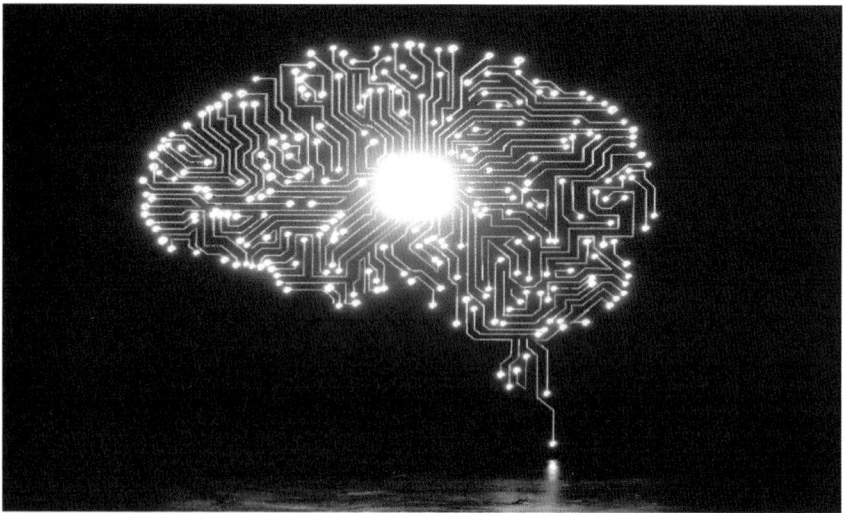

2. Emotions and Feelings:

Emotions are like colorful clouds that float around in your brain. There are happy clouds, sad clouds, and even angry clouds. These clouds make you feel different things. When you're happy, it's like a sunny day in your brain! And when you're sad, it's like a cloudy day.

Activity time: Use a blank paper and draw colorful clouds that float around in your brain

3. Breathing and Emotions:

But here's the exciting part! You can help your brain control those emotions, especially when you want to feel calm or happy. It's all about something called 'breathing.' When you breathe, you give your brain special powers to calm down the stormy clouds and make them happy again!

4. The Breathing Sequence:

Are you ready to learn a special sequence to calm your feelings? Let's do it together:

a. **Take a deep breath:** Breathe in slowly through your nose like you're smelling a beautiful flower. Feel your tummy rise as you breathe in.

b. **Hold your breath:** Now, hold your breath for a second, like you're making a wish.

c. **Breathe out:** Gently breathe out through your mouth, like you're blowing out a birthday candle. Feel your tummy go down as you breathe out.

d. **Repeat:** Do this **three times** or more, like a magic spell, and watch how your feelings start to calm down."

So, remember kids, your brain is like a superhero, and you can help it control your feelings with your magical breath. Now that we've practiced our particular sequence, let's start reading our fun book and doing our activities with calm and happy hearts!"

Draw or Colour YOUR own superhero costumes

Let us begin .....

CHAPTER 1

SEÁN FROM THE STARS: A SUPERHERO'S JOURNEY TO HIS NEW HOME

Once upon a time, in the quiet village of Ballybrook, there lived a young superhero named Seán, who was not your ordinary boy. Seán hailed from the distant planet of Krypton, but he had moved to Earth to live among humans. His Kryptonian name was Síofra, but here on Earth, everyone called him Seán.

Seán's arrival in Ballybrook was quite extraordinary. He had been sent to Earth to escape the troubles on his home planet. As he landed in his spaceship, he was overwhelmed by the new sights, sounds, and people. His eyes sparkled with a twinkle of stars, and his dark hair gleamed like the night sky.

At first, Seán felt like an alien, so different from the Earth children. He could run faster than the wind, leap higher than the tallest trees, and have super strength. His powers made it challenging for him to fit in, but he longed to make friends.

One sunny day, while at the local park, Seán saw a group of

children playing. He watched them from afar, and his heart ached to join in their games. Bravely, he approached them, introducing himself with a friendly, "Hello, I'm Seán."

The children were fascinated by his unique abilities, and soon, they all became friends. He showed them his incredible powers, like flying high above the clouds, and they were in awe. Seán's new friends, Aoife, Cian, and Siobhán, were kind and accepting. They quickly realized that, even though Seán was different, he had a heart of gold and was a true friend.

As the days turned into weeks and months, Seán and his friends had many adventures. They helped Seán learn about Earth and its customs while he shared stories of his life on Krypton. Seán taught his friends about the importance of kindness and always being there for one another, just like his old friends from back home.

Seán's extraordinary powers soon became a secret only his friends knew, and they felt like they had their own superhero. They loved having him as a friend, and together, they made Ballybrook a better place, helping those in need and protecting their village.

But Seán never forgot about his old friends on Krypton. He sent messages to them through the stars, showing them the beauty of Earth and the wonderful friends he had made. He was able to bridge the gap between his old life and his new one, proving that true friendship knows no boundaries, not even those between different planets.

Seán, Aoife, Cian, and Siobhán remained the best of friends as the years went by. They knew that being different could be a superpower in itself and that true friends would always be there for you, no matter where you came from. Seán's journey from the far reaches of space to the heart of Ballybrook had taught them all a valuable lesson: with kindness, acceptance, and a little bit of superpower, you can make the best of friends, even in the most unexpected of places.

Activity time

Use some paper to jot down what sets you apart and makes you unique, and embrace and take pride in your uniqueness.

CHAPTER 2

LEXI AND THE MAGIC OF SELF-LOVE: A FAIRY TALE ADVENTURE

Once upon a time, in the charming town of Everville, there were four best friends named Lexi, Jack, Emma, and Oliver. They all loved to gather under the giant oak tree in the park after school to listen to their favorite storyteller, Grandma Ellie.

One sunny afternoon, Grandma Ellie began a tale about self-love, using their beloved fairy tale characters. "Once in the magical kingdom of Joyland," she began, "there lived a gentle, kind-hearted fairy named Ruby."

Lexi, who was the most curious of the group, asked, "But why was Ruby so special, Grandma?"

"Well," Grandma Ellie continued, "Ruby was special because she knew how to love herself. She didn't just help others, but she also knew how to be kind and gentle with herself. In the kingdom, there was a mirror of truth that revealed one's inner feelings, and Ruby's mirror always shone with a warm and bright light."

The children listened intently as Grandma Ellie continued the story. "In Joyland, there was another fairy named Sam, who was always trying to be someone he wasn't. He thought he needed to look like the strongest fairy in the land, with the brightest wings. But deep inside, he was unhappy because he wasn't being true to himself."

Jack, the most adventurous of the group, asked, "What happened next, Grandma Ellie?"

"Well," Grandma Ellie replied, "one day, a great challenge came to Joyland. A dragon had captured the magical flowers that kept the kingdom happy. Ruby, being the kind fairy she was, decided to help, and she asked Sam to join her."

The story unfolded as Ruby and Sam embarked on their adventure. Through their journey, Sam discovered that by embracing his true self and accepting his strengths and weaknesses, he became a more powerful and happy fairy.

Emma, who was known for her wisdom, said, "So, Grandma Ellie, self-love is about accepting who you are?"

Grandma Ellie nodded and smiled, "That's right, Emma. Loving yourself means embracing your uniqueness, strengths, and weaknesses. When you truly love yourself, you become a source of light and happiness for everyone around you."

The children understood the story's message, and they each

promised to be more like Ruby, spreading love and kindness to others while also remembering to love and be kind to themselves. And so, under the giant oak tree, the four friends learned the importance of self-love through the enchanting world of fairy tales guided by the wise and wonderful Grandma Ellie.

Activity time:

Let's go Outdoor! Spelling Hopscotch:

- Draw a hopscotch grid with letters instead of numbers.

-Spell a word by hopping from one letter to another, making learning a physical activity.

CHAPTER 3
THE STARRY NIGHT ADVENTURE – LIGHTS OUT.

Once upon a time, in a small, cosy town, there lived a little boy named Timmy who was terribly afraid of sleeping in the dark. Every night, he would ask his parents to keep the lights on, and they would, but he knew it couldn't last forever. Timmy's parents decided it was time to help him overcome his fear.

One evening, as the sun began to set, Timmy's mom sat him down on his bed. She said, "Timmy, I have a special story to tell you. It's about a magical adventure you can go on every night." Timmy's eyes widened with curiosity.

His mom continued, "You see, there's a magical world that comes alive when it's dark outside. It's called the 'Starry Night Adventure.' In this world, you can embark on the most amazing journeys with the help of your imagination."

Timmy was intrigued. "But how do I get there, Mom?"

His dad joined in, "You don't need to go anywhere. You can visit this world right from your own room. All you need to do is close your eyes, take a deep breath, and start to dream."

Timmy tried it that very night. He closed his eyes and took a deep breath. In his mind's eye, he saw a path leading into a dark forest. As he ventured deeper, he noticed the stars above shining like little nightlights, lighting his way.

He met friendly creatures like the "Glowing Fireflies," who guided him with their soft, warm light. He played with the "Shadow Puppets" that danced on his bedroom walls, and they made him giggle.

As the nights passed, Timmy's fear of the dark began to fade away. He looked forward to his "Starry Night Adventure" and all the exciting places he could explore. The more he believed in the magic, the brighter the stars shone in his imaginary world.

One night, as he lay in bed, Timmy realized that he no longer needed the lights on in his room. He had his own special, starry friends to keep him company, and he felt safe in their soft, gentle glow.

From that day on, Timmy's room became his gateway to the "Starry Night Adventure," and he learned that there was nothing to fear in the dark. He had found the magic in his imagination, making him brave and strong.

And so, the little boy who was once scared of sleeping in the dark became the bravest adventurer in the "Starry Night

Adventure" world, inspiring other children to embrace the magic of their own imaginations and conquer their fears.

A calming breathing technique can benefit children when it's time to sleep. Here's a simple and child-friendly breathing exercise that can aid relaxation and promote better sleep:

Note for the adult who will help you practice: This Sleepy Starfish Breathing Technique helps children slow down and relax, making it easier for them to fall asleep. It engages their imagination and encourages a calm, rhythmic breathing pattern that's perfect for bedtime. You can practice this with your child until they become comfortable doing it independently.

Step 1: Lie Down Comfortably
Lie in your bed or on a comfy surface, like a cosy blanket or mat. Could you make sure you're in a relaxed position?

Step 2: Close Your Eyes
Please close your eyes to help you focus on your breathing and imagination.

Step 3: Imagine Being a Starfish
Imagine that you are a sleepy starfish resting on a quiet, sandy beach. Picture the soft sand and the gentle waves lapping at the shore.

Step 4: Inhale Slowly and Deeply
Take a slow, deep breath in through their nose. As you breathe in, ask them to imagine the starfish's arms gently opening and stretching.

Step 5: Hold Your Breath

After inhaling, have them hold their breath for just a moment. During this pause, picture the starfish pausing to enjoy the calmness of the beach.

Step 6: Exhale Slowly and Completely

Now, exhale slowly through their mouth, imagining the starfish's arms gently closing back together. As you breathe out, you can imagine any worries or busy thoughts being carried away by the waves.

Step 7: Repeat

Repeat this breathing pattern, inhaling slowly, holding for a moment, and exhaling slowly. They can do this for a few minutes or as long as they need to feel relaxed and sleepy.

Step 8: Drift into Dreamland

Imagine themselves drifting off to sleep on the peaceful beach as a starfish, feeling safe and cosy.

CHAPTER 4
THE SUPER HELPERS

Three exceptional children with extraordinary abilities lived in the picturesque town of Sevilla. Their names were Carlos, Maria, and Juan, and they had an important message to share.

Carlos was a curious boy who loved to learn, but one day, he faced challenging math homework. The fractions seemed like a puzzle he couldn't solve. Luckily, his friend Maria, known for her super math skills, arrived just in time. She made math exciting, turning fractions into a fun adventure. With Maria's help, Carlos completed his homework with a smile.

Juan was the star player on the soccer field, but recently, he had been struggling to score goals. He felt frustrated and was about to give up. That's when "Speedster" appeared. Speedster could run faster than the wind and offered to train Juan. With Speedster's guidance and support, Juan regained his confidence and became the team's top scorer.

One sunny afternoon, a big shoelace-tying competition was happening in town, and Pablo, the reigning champion, was nervous. He couldn't remember how to tie his laces quickly. In his time of need, "Elastica" appeared. Elastica had stretchy arms and showed Pablo the secret to tying laces in the blink of an eye. With her guidance, Pablo won the competition and set a new record.

These three kids, along with their superhero friends, realized the power of working together and asking for help. They joined forces and became "The Spanish Super Helpers," a team dedicated to supporting one another and their community.

The Spanish Super Helpers soon understood that asking for help was not a sign of weakness but a strength. They proudly proclaimed their motto: "Super Friends Stick Together." Their story spread throughout the town, inspiring others to seek assistance when needed and reminding everyone that we all have our unique strengths and superpowers. Together, we can overcome any challenge.

Activity time

Ask an adult to help with this activity

Sensory Spelling Trays:
- Fill shallow trays with various materials like sand, salt, or colored rice.
- Use YOUR finger to write spelling words in the material, which provides a tactile learning experience.

CHAPTER 5
LILY & THE FAIRY OF FRIENDSHIP

Once upon a time, a young girl named Lily lived in a magical land. Lily was kind-hearted and loved spending time with her friends. However, lately, she has been feeling left out and hurt by her friends, just like the Seven Dwarfs in the story of Sleeping Beauty.

One sunny morning, as Lily sat beneath her favorite tree, feeling sad and lonely, a gentle voice called out to her. It was the Fairy of Friendship who had noticed Lily's distress. The fairy understood Lily's troubles and wanted to help her.

"My dear Lily," said the Fairy of Friendship, "I have a special tale to share with you. It's a story about a brave princess who faced challenges with her friendship group, just like you. Are you ready to embark on this magical journey?"

Lily's eyes lit up with curiosity and hope. She nodded eagerly, ready to hear the tale that would touch her heart and bring her solace.

Once upon a time, there was a princess named Ann, much like Sleeping Beauty. She had a close-knit group of friends who were like the Seven Dwarfs. Each dwarf had a unique personality, just like Lily's friends. However, like Lily, Ann started feeling excluded and left out of her friendship group.

The first dwarf, Happy, always seemed busy and rarely had time for Ann. She felt saddened by his absence and wondered if she had done something wrong. The second dwarf, Grumpy, often snapped at her and made her doubt herself. Ann felt hurt by his words, as Lily did by her friends' actions.

While Ann was feeling downhearted, she discovered a secret path in the enchanted forest one day. She followed it and stumbled upon a magical garden. In the garden, she found a mirror reflecting her true self and strengths. The mirror revealed that true friends accept and appreciate each other for who they are.

Ann journeyed through the garden and encountered a wise owl who guided her. The owl shared valuable lessons about friendship and reminded Ann that she deserved friends who treated her with kindness and respect. Ann realised that her true worth was not defined by how others treated her but by how she treated herself.

Empowered by this newfound wisdom, Ann spoke honestly with her friends. She expressed her feelings and explained how their actions had hurt her. To Ann's surprise, her friends listened carefully and genuinely cared about her well-being. They apologised and promised to make amends.

Together, they learned the importance of communication, empathy, and understanding in a strong friendship. They promised to support and uplift each other, embracing their differences and celebrating their unique qualities.

Lily listened intently to the story, feeling a sense of hope fill her heart. She realised that, just like Ann, she could find her inner strength and have open conversations with her friends. She understood that true friends would listen and try to make amends, just as Ann's friends had done.

With newfound courage and understanding, Lily reached out to her friends. She shared her feelings honestly, just as Ann had done, and to her joy, her friends were receptive and understanding. They apologised for their unintentional neglect and reassured her of their friendship.

From that day forward, Lily and her friends grew closer than ever before. They learned to appreciate and value each other's unique qualities, just like Ann and the Seven Dwarfs had done. And in their newfound unity, they created a friendship that was even stronger and more magical than before.

As Lily closed her eyes, she thanked the Fairy of Friendship for the tale. She felt inspired to nurture her friendships and cherish the bonds she shared with her friends. With the lessons from the story of Ann and the Seven Dwarfs, Lily knew that she would overcome her challenges and create a happier, more inclusive friendship group. And so, Lily's heart filled with hope as she embraced her own magical journey of friendship and self-discovery.

Activity time:

Word Family Treasure Hunt

Preparation:
- Create word family cards (e.g., -at, -en, -ing) with words and pictures.
- Hide these cards around your home or in the backyard, making sure they're well concealed but accessible.

How to Play:
- Explain to the children or your friends, that they are going on a treasure hunt to discover hidden word family cards.
- Provide an example: "If you find the -at card, you can make words like 'cat,' 'bat,' and 'mat.'"
- Equip the child with a small bag or basket for their treasures.
- Encourage them to explore and find as many cards as they can.
- Once they've collected a handful of cards, bring them together and create words using the word family.

This exciting activity combines the joy of discovery with word building, making it a delightful and educational outdoor game for children and even the whole family to enjoy.

CHAPTER 6

THE BRAVE LITTLE PRINCESS

Once upon a time, in the enchanted kingdom of Serenità, there lived a brave little princess named Sofia. Despite her royal status, Sofia was no ordinary princess. She had a kind heart and a curious mind, leading her on countless adventures.

One sunny morning, Sofia ventured into the depths of the Foresta Incantata, guided by a desire to understand the well-being of the children in her kingdom. She had noticed many children feeling anxious and wanted to find a way to help them.

As she journeyed through the forest, she stumbled upon a hidden cottage, its door slightly ajar. Cautiously, she opened it and discovered a room filled with colorful books. One particular book caught her attention— A collection of ancient fairy tales that contained the wisdom of past generations.

With a spark of inspiration, Sofia began reading each tale,

searching for answers. The stories spoke of courage, resilience, and the importance of self-belief. She realised that these enchanting tales held valuable lessons for the children of Serenità.

Determined to share the wisdom she had gained, Princess Sofia organised a festival of stories in the castle gardens. Children from all corners of the kingdom gathered their faces filled with anticipation. The princess took centre stage, holding the magical book in her hands.

She started with the story of "The Little Engine That Could," teaching the children that they could overcome any obstacle with perseverance and a positive mindset. Next, she told the tale of "The Ugly Duckling," reminding the children that they are unique and beautiful, no matter what others may say.

From that day forward, Princess Sofia made storytelling a regular event in the kingdom. Children would gather monthly to listen to stories and learn important life lessons. The magical stories comforted children, helping them overcome their fears and nurture their well-being.

Activity time

Create a short story about something that makes you feel happy. You can share it with others to make them feel happy, too.

CHAPTER 7

THE UNSEEN GUARDIAN

In the mystical realm of Evergreen, a young fairy named Willow flitted about, her wings shimmering with shades of emerald. Willow had a special gift—she could see and sense the emotions of all living beings, including the children of Evergreen. One evening, as Willow glided through the moonlit forest, she noticed a dark cloud lingering over the village. The children's laughter had faded, replaced by hushed whispers and worried expressions. Concerned, Willow knew it was her duty to discover the source of their anxiety. Guided by her intuition, Willow followed a winding path that led her to a secluded grove. Nestled in the centre was an ancient oak tree, known as the Tree of Whispers. It's gnarled branches whispered secrets and held the collective wisdom of the forest. With a flutter of her wings, Willow perched on a branch and shared her worries with the Tree.

The ancient oak rustled its leaves, revealing a hidden realm where fairy tales came to life. It was a place where children's dreams and fears intertwined, shaping their well-being. Determined to aid the children, Willow ventured into the realm of stories. She encountered a young boy named Samuel, whose fear of the dark held him captive every night. Willow reached out her hand, and together, they embarked on a journey through the story of "Little Red Riding Hood."

As they weaved through the tale, Willow unveiled the hidden messages beneath the surface. She showed Samuel how Little Red's bravery and cleverness helped her overcome her fears. Samuel's eyes widened with understanding, and a glimmer of courage sparked within him. Encouraged by their success, Willow continued to help other children. She accompanied a girl named Amelia through the tale of "Cinderella," teaching her the importance of self-worth and the power of kindness. The children's anxieties melted away with each story, replaced by newfound strength and resilience. Word of Willow's wondrous gift spread throughout Evergreen. Children sought her guidance, and together, they delved into the realms of fairy tales, exploring their fears and emerging with hope. The unseen guardian, Willow, became a symbol of comfort, reminding the children that they were never alone in their struggles.

As seasons passed, the clouds of anxiety dissipated, and laughter once again filled the village of Evergreen. The children thrived, armed with the wisdom of fairy tales and the knowledge that their emotions were valid. Willow, the guardian of well-being, watched over them with a heart brimming with joy and pride.

Activity time:

Here's a riddle based on the story of "The Unseen Guardian."

CLUE: The answer to the riddle is a word that relates to the story:

I'm a magical friend in Evergreen's land,
With wings so bright, I lend a helping hand.
In whispers and leaves, I seek tales untold,
To heal children's hearts, I am ever so bold.

Who am I?

CHAPTER 8
HEROES OF THE HEART: EMBRACING OUR SUPERPOWERS

Once upon a time, a group of extraordinary children lived in the vibrant city of Happyville. They were just like any other kids their age, attending the local school and playing in the park. However, each of them possessed a unique superpower that made them special.

First, there was Emily, a shy and quiet girl who had the power of empathy. She could feel and understand other people's emotions, comforting those in need. Despite her power, Emily often felt unnoticed and unimportant.

Then, there was William, a boy who could control plants and make them grow with a single touch. William loved nature and had a green thumb, but he struggled with self-doubt, thinking that his power was insignificant compared to his friends' abilities.

Charlotte was another group member, a fearless girl with the power of super speed. She could run faster than anyone, making her the perfect hero to save the day. However, Charlotte often felt lonely and disconnected because she thought her speed set her apart from her friends.

Lastly, there was Benjamin, a boy with the power of telekinesis. He could move objects with his mind, which was incredibly cool, but Benjamin struggled with feelings of inadequacy because he believed his power wasn't flashy enough.

One sunny day, a special event was taking place in Happyville—the Great Heroes' Parade. The children were excited to watch their favorite heroes display their incredible powers and inspire them with acts of bravery. But as they sat on the sidelines, they couldn't help but feel a tinge of sadness, longing to be up there, feeling important and valued.

As they watched, the heroes, Emily, William, Charlotte, and Benjamin, realized that their powers, though different from the flashy ones they admired, were just as meaningful. They realized that true worth comes from within, not from external validation.

With newfound determination, the four friends decided to put their unique abilities to use. Emily used her empathy to comfort a friend who was feeling down, reminding them that they were loved and supported. William cultivated a small garden in the park, bringing beauty and joy to those who passed by. Charlotte used her incredible speed to help an elderly neighbor with their chores, making their day a little easier. Benjamin used his telekinesis to organize a charity event, lifting heavy objects effortlessly and creating a sense of unity within the community.

Word of their extraordinary acts of kindness quickly spread throughout Happyville. People were inspired by the children's selflessness and the positive impact they had on others' lives. The Great Heroes' Parade organizers even invited them to join the parade as honorary heroes.

When the day of the parade arrived, Emily, William, Charlotte, and Benjamin proudly marched alongside their favorite heroes, feeling a sense of self-worth that they had never experienced before. They realized that being a hero wasn't just about flashy powers but about using their unique gifts to make the world a better place and bring joy to those around them.

From that day forward, the four friends continued to embrace their powers and spread kindness wherever they went. They discovered that true self-worth comes from within and that everyone has the power to make a difference, no matter how big or small their abilities may seem.

And so, in the city of Happyville, Emily, William, Charlotte, and Benjamin became known as the Heroes of the Heart, teaching everyone the valuable lesson that true worth lies in the power of kindness, and empathy, and using their unique strengths to bring happiness to others.

Activity time:

Let's get your imagination working.

Draw a picture of you as a superhero and what powers you would hold.

CHAPTER 9

HOW LENNY LEARNED TO LEAP OVER LANGUAGE

Once upon a time, on the rolling green hills of Meadowvale, there lived a curious young lamb named Lenny. Lenny was a spirited and imaginative lamb with dreams of one day becoming a great scholar. Every day, he'd watch the other animals in the meadow and admire their various talents. The cows were excellent at growing the juiciest clover, the rabbits hopped and skipped in rhythmic harmony, and the ducks swam in perfect formation. Lenny, however, had a little problem that made him feel different from the rest.

One sunny morning, as the meadow was bathed in golden sunlight, the wise old sheep, Miss Ewe, gathered all the young animals under the shade of the towering oak tree. She announced, "Today, my dear students, we will be reading our favorite book, 'The Animal Farm Chronicles.' This book is filled with wisdom and knowledge. It's time for you all to read a page aloud."

Lenny's heart sank. He had trouble reading, and this particular book was full of big, complicated words. The other animals seemed so confident, effortlessly reading their parts. The cows mooed the words melodiously, the rabbits hopped through the sentences, and the ducks quacked the verses beautifully.

Lenny felt a sense of unease. How could he read in front of everyone when he stumbled over even the simplest words? Miss Ewe called Lenny to read, and he nervously stammered through the first sentence. The animals began to giggle, and Lenny's face turned as pink as a freshly bloomed rose. He wished he could sink into the ground.

As the days went by, Lenny found himself growing more anxious and discouraged. He stopped attending school and spent his time alone in the meadow, feeling isolated and sad. He yearned to be like the other animals, but he couldn't see a way to overcome his reading difficulties.

One sunny afternoon, while Lenny was sitting by the pond, he noticed a group of ants working tirelessly to build a bridge across the water. Lenny admired their teamwork and perseverance, and he decided to approach them.

"Excuse me, little ants," Lenny said, "I can see you're all good at working together to achieve your goal. Could you help me too?"

The ants, without hesitation, agreed to help Lenny. They knew they weren't the biggest or the strongest, but they were excellent builders. They guided Lenny through the words, one by one, patiently teaching him how to read and pronounce them correctly. Lenny, with the help of the ants, soon gained confidence in his reading abilities.

As the days passed, Lenny improved significantly. He returned to school with newfound enthusiasm and read with more confidence than ever before. The other animals noticed his progress and were amazed by his determination. Lenny realized that everyone had their unique strengths and weaknesses, just like the animals in the meadow. It was okay to ask for help when you needed it.

At the end of the school year, Miss Ewe decided to celebrate the achievements of her students by organizing a grand performance of 'The Animal Farm Chronicles.' Lenny, with the ants' support, was chosen to recite the book's prologue. He stood before the audience, took a deep breath, and spoke the words clearly and confidently, just like he had always wanted to.

The meadow filled with applause, and the other animals realized the importance of helping one another. They understood that everyone had different talents and abilities, and by working together and asking for help when needed, they could achieve great things.

And so, the moral of the story is this: It's okay to ask for help, for in the meadow of life, we are all unique and special in our own way. By embracing our differences and focusing on our strengths, we can overcome challenges and achieve greatness, just like Lenny the Lamb.

Activity time:

The activity-based techniques below will help YOU develop reading and spelling skills and make learning an interactive and enjoyable experience.

Creating activity-based reading and spelling techniques for children can make learning more engaging and enjoyable. Here's a set of activities to help children improve their reading and spelling skills:

Rhyming Bingo
- Create rhyming bingo cards with pictures and words (e.g., cat, hat, bat).
- Play rhyming bingo, where the child matches words that rhyme.

Spelling Bee Relay
- Organize a spelling bee relay race with friends or family members.
- Each participant spells a word, and the team with the correct spellings wins the race.

Story Stones
- Paint or draw pictures on stones or pebbles representing characters, objects, and actions.
- Encourage the child to arrange the stones to create a story and read it aloud

ANSWER TO THE RIDDLE:

> I'm a magical friend in Evergreen's land,
> With wings so bright, I lend a helping hand.
> In whispers and leaves, I seek tales untold,
> To heal children's hearts, I am ever so bold.
>
> Who am I? (Answer: Willow)

Printed in Great Britain
by Amazon